Critical Praise

Out of Violence into Poetry by Ma[...] height of poetry written in any lang[...] in the last hundred years and constitutes the broadest, most ge[...] penetrating and most profound gamble on the part of an extraordinary human being, an extraordinary life and work, on that which we call *future*. This book—concrete, situated, tangible in its truth and commitment, in its fierce and corrosive irony and public kindness and compassion—creates a fresco that is at once compendium and legacy. This is true from the first poem, "Portrait of the Artist as an Old Woman," to the last line of the one that ends the collection, "Promising Trouble When I'm Gone." Here are the most penetrating and powerful metaphors that a book of poetry can give us in the unending second-to-second struggle that millions of people across the face of the earth wage in order to become fully human and continue to be so. Only a great poet, a poet of Margaret Randall's magnitude, could title her book *Out of Violence into Poetry* and include in it one of the most moving poems I have had the privilege of reading: "I Celebrate." No one who reads or writes will be able to diminish this poetic triumph. As with all great works, no one could have imagined something like it could have been written. And yet it was. Thank you, Margaret Randall.

—Raul Zurita, Chile's National Literature Prize (2000)
and the Pablo Neruda Award (1988)

Ever courageous, in these poems *de memoria,* Margaret Randall faces this hour of plague looking back at catastrophes that ravaged Mexico, Cuba and Central America in her younger days. She upholds the "mystery that catches light…but something is lost, fashioned of blood and memory." As witness, writer, mother and revolutionary, she marshals a confidence: "I never doubted / I would do it all." Yet in nightmares she is endlessly looking for a passport before a flight to Cuba. In spite of the closing door of her time, she sees "a future gripped by the music of wings." She is undeterred at 84. A tribute she writes for a friend—that death "doesn't close a door, your name / remains a fierce marker" —describes her own valor and integrity.

—Renny Golden, author of *The Music of Her Rivers*

These poems are like a shield. As one reads them, they become a gentle sailboat plowing the Southern seas as a few fish, algae, moons and stones leap around it—thrown against its timeless journey—its primary nourishment. The sun beyond. An itinerant beating heart, out of violence into poetry.

—Nancy Morejón, National Literature Prize, Cuba 2001

Reading Margaret Randall's new book, *Out of Violence into Poetry*, affirmed not only my intellectual understanding of it but it was also a deeply emotional experience for me. The literary dynamic of being human is complex, intense, extensive—and seemingly limitless—and at times the human soul-spirit may feel overly challenged. Human expression is as vast as human experience and, in this book not every word, feeling, focus, view is acceptable to all, but that is poetry. I highly recommend reading Randall's poetry.

—Simon J. Ortiz, Acoma poet-writer, Lifetime Achievement Award from the Native Writers Circle of the Americas

Now in her ninth decade, Margaret Randall is a poet at the height of her power, and nowhere is this more evident than in the pages of *Out of Violence into Poetry.* Randall's voice is "resonant, neither / battered by age / nor strained by circumstance." She is a sure and steady guide through political upheaval, state-sanctioned violence, global pandemic, and the long arc of our collective history. Though, like poetry itself, Randall "never said / I'd change the world," the offerings in this collection might just shorten the distance between "us and them," between the promise of the human race and the reality that leaves so many to "only hope for survival." Like poetry, Randall is here "trying my best, / and you might do me the favor / of appreciating me for what I am." And how we do.

—Michelle Otero, author of *Bosque: Poems*

OUT OF VIOLENCE

INTO POETRY

OUT OF VIOLENCE INTO POETRY

POEMS 2018–2021

MARGARET RANDALL

SAN ANTONIO, TEXAS
2021

Out of Violence into Poetry

Cover art, "Lower Antelope Canyon"
photograph by Margaret Randall

First Edition
ISBN: 978-1-60940-619-6

E-books:
ISBN: 978-1-60940-620-2

Wings Press
P.O. Box 591176
San Antonio, Texas 78259

Wings Press books are distributed to the trade by
Independent Publishers Group
www.ipgbook.com

Due to the 2020 pandemic, no Library of Congress
cataloging-in-publication data was available.

for Barbara, in a time of plague

that you have made easier with

your wisdom and your love.

Contents

OUT OF VIOLENCE

INTO POETRY

Portrait of the Artist as an Old Woman

Words and images keep showing up.
I manage a quick sidestep
to let them pass
but cannot avoid collision.

Waiting at the doctor or dentist's
I thumb through a worn magazine.
Ideas leap from its pages:
arrows snagging memory.

In the supermarket foreign foods aisle,
on labels I cannot read and boxes
I'll never purchase, coded phrases
act as if they belong to me.

Driving across high desert, piñon and sage
for miles on either side,
I pull off road, grab pen and paper
and begin.

And looking in a mirror or running
from myself, I imagine a portrait
of the artist as an old woman,
in past tense and sure future.

I pause to soak up sun or hide in the shade
of someone else's story. The poem
is always waiting around the corner
ready to tell me who I am.

I Celebrate

for Michelle Otero

Let me celebrate this cobalt sky, blazing
desert fire and red rock canyons
revealing messages from those who went before,
the stories they tell as I listen
to their wonder and their warnings.

I celebrate each child, grandchild and
greatgrandchild, human lines
of personhood I follow in loops feeding
back to myself, astonished and grateful
as I trace my oldest questions on their lips.

I celebrate the woman who walks beside me,
beloved companion on this journey,
artist's eye and perfect temperature of skin,
crinkling laugh lines about her eyes
that see too much and just enough.

I celebrate my own worn body, wrinkles
and sag where muscle once held forth,
this body that still serves and energizes,
sustaining the weight of memory,
bringing it home in grace.

And I celebrate memory itself, playful
trickster, fusion of pain and joy,
ribbon of indelible moments that nourish
me in the lonely times
and through the empty spaces.

Rejoicing in these words I birth, I celebrate
my peoples' cries, our song's weave
even as it may taunt me, hide or murmur
behind my back, chatter incoherently as
my voice becomes part of its warp and weft.

I celebrate our indelible grief, hard knots
bursting with scattered tendrils of hope.
Beyond these shadows of avarice and sickness,
racist hate and twisted power I celebrate
each victory as we bring it forth.

One Tectonic Plate Slipping Beneath Another

for Barrett and Robin

It was a continent, robust with mountains
and deserts, alive with a song
that promised forever.

But the land suddenly rifted, one tectonic plate
slipping beneath another, threatening
to take you with it into oblivion

to a place where sound becomes sight
and then again sound,
familiars flee your spirit

leaving you adrift
where nothing
is what it was. Nothing.

Until, floating in that same sea, someone
always there in the wings
swims up beside you,

takes your hand, looks into your eyes
and tells you it's okay
to start again. Yes, she says, late

as it is. Yes, she smiles without need
of words. Yes and yes in this
other life that couldn't have predicted itself.

Out of Violence into Poetry

Water, real or illusory, shimmers along
the desert horizon.
Oasis: early 17th century word
via late Latin from the Greek,
perhaps of Egyptian origin.

Egypt, a country of vast sand
where wet and fertile
exceptions nourish life.
Also: peaceful area or period
in the midst of troubled times.

Thus, place becomes time in the blink
of geography's eye.
Double helix embracing itself
as it rises in our throats:
see-saw of intuition singing loud.

Let me satiate your thirst, feed
your hunger. Satisfy mine,
if only because we are
conscious beings standing together
in this dangerous century.

We are reduced to small gestures:
reflected in a gaze
or touch of a hand,
oases of light where we may move
out of violence into poetry.

Voice

Voice said what it was born to say
even when high school teacher
father and husband
took pains to contain it.

Pains: exemplary, decorated ones.
You wouldn't know it though.
Impossible to go against
such forces of nature.

Voice snuggled between the sheets
wouldn't eat its vegetables
sounded high-pitched
sometimes landed with a thud.

But its name was Voice and it grew
to meet every challenge
fill every space
build a bit of victory in your mouth.

What They So Generously Bestow

I swipe my foot this way and that
across curbstone or threshold
trying to disengage what holds tight
to the sole of my shoe,
won't let go.

At times it feels like diamonds
in a little satin drawstring bag
or some ancient treasure
acquired at a spice market
in a city along the Silk Road.

At times I know it is trash
pretending value,
sticking to me like a wad
of toilet paper as I exit
a public restroom.

The unknown and unwanted
begins to weigh me down.
I cannot rid myself of its bulk.
I am limping now
into forbidden future.

Too often we get what we
don't ask for
because the givers are sure
anyone would be happy to have
what they so generously bestow.

The Being Who Lives in Our Desire

I can remember the label *illegitimate*
shaming a child
whose father didn't recognize
his part in bringing him to life,
years when uncertain gender was decided
by a doctor guided by the size of genitalia,
assumption of male or female identity
imperative from birth.

In my childhood loving someone
of the same sex
wasn't on our list of choices.
We hid in shadows moving
in and out of shame and liberation,
places where we pretended to be ourselves
as long as unobtrusive,
inoffensive to the Others.

I don't care what you do in private
the rule-makers lied
just so you don't flaunt it in my face.
As long as boys could be boys
and girls remain subservient
to their demands.
Clear gender categories
like acceptable class and color lines.

Today the fictitious binary collapses
beneath its demeaning weight
as we transition to that being

who lives in our desire, risk
murder born of macho insecurity
but request the pronoun
that feels comfortable,
insist you acknowledge who we are.

On the Botswana savannah five lionesses
toss unlikely manes.
In an all-male school of clownfish
one becomes female to reproduce.
Female and male hyenas
have testes and a penis.
But wait, that's not a penis
but a clitoris larger than any male organ.

I cannot tell which androgynous roadrunner
is male, female or of another gender
among those that visit me
as spring moves into summer
and imprisoning conformity
gives way to a recognition
of the range of difference swelling
the unexpected colors of our rainbow.

Today Was a Good Day

Today was a good day. To begin with
I woke up this morning
and was able to get out of bed
unbending the length of my body.

I could aim a remote at the heater
and the room began
to lose its chill. The milk
in my refrigerator hadn't gone bad.

If I opened my door I wouldn't
find myself in Mogadishu
or Bagdad.
New Mexico's sun holds me close.

My children nurture their children
in cities where life is possible.
The ravages of hunger haven't yet
claimed their limbs and eyes.

It is easy to calculate solutions
to the world's problems
nestled on a comfortable couch
or seated before a computer.

I know I must consult the mother
forced back to Honduras
without her child, the young girl
taken by Boko Haram.

I understand the distance
I'd have to travel,
the languages I'd have to learn
to be free from "them" and "me."

Today was a good day but even if
just some of the walls come down
it will be better tomorrow,
better still the next.

Banana. Sunrise. Chair.

I'll say three words, the nurse explains,
and I want you to repeat them
after me.
Later I'll ask you to tell me
what they were.
She says three words
and I repeat them
then wait complacently
for the next problem.

Banana. Sunrise. Chair. I try
to remember those words
as I draw a picture of a clock
at ten past eleven, make a circle,
then place a 12 at the top,
6 at the bottom, 3 and 9 where they go
before filling in the other numbers.
I draw the small hand pointing
at 11, the long aimed at 2.

Excellent, the nurse smiles
as she takes the paper
from my hand,
then waits a moment
before asking me
for the three words.
I say banana and sunrise,
think a moment
before adding chair.

I wonder why I hesitated
before chair, what
this test says about my memory
today or tomorrow
and how important it is
to be able to remember three words
or draw a clock with its numbers
in the right places,
hands spelling 10 past 11.

I don't need to be reminded of the touch
of your hand against my cheek,
the way your skin feels against mine,
its temperature and breath.
I hope I never forget these things
no nurse asks.
Banana and *sunrise* and *chair*
take up dubious residence in me:
imposters defeated before the game ends.

Lifetime Warranty

Age wears on the body parts
and I imagine a shop
where replacements are shelved
by model and date,
the experimental or mass-produced
on special sales tables
daring us to try a plastic nose
immune to sun damage
or super batteries for heart or liver
guaranteed to last forever.

Generic models would attract
the low-income shopper,
luxury versions the elite who
have everything but a perfect working body.
The dispensary itself might be
an upscale boutique or big box store
where everyone goes for bargains
though no remedies yet for serious cancers,
dementia or flesh-eating bacteria.

Short-term solutions are advertised
in glowing terms and offered
on brightly decorated racks
right beside the cashier:
They just may get you on the way out
and there is no layaway.
This month's special
is portable oxygen in tropical flavors.
No shortage of deception when hope wears thin.

I imagine visiting such a futuristic shop,
boutique or bargain basement,
and know it's a First World dream.
Desperate people everywhere
sell body parts: hair and kidneys,
or use their organs to carry contraband.
If lucky they may get enough to eat
for a few more months,
a fleeting chance at another day.

What would a lifetime warranty mean
to a body wearing only hope?
Will the consumer hold out for designer DNA
or invest in replacement body parts?
How can those who sell a piece of themselves
be sure a sliver of spirit or strand of character
isn't lost in that deal of last resort?
Privilege stalks the rich
while the poor hope only for survival.

The Loneliness of Age

My shadow fails to accompany me
or be a good enough companion,
the sort of friend who keeps
the conversation going,
talks back when I need
to test an idea
or play to a worthy opponent.

Where I once held a child to breast
a cold wind chills.
The loneliness of age
inhabits no temperature
I have known
as it marks time to the beat
of diminishing confidence.

I send out telepathic messages,
close my eyes
and almost stumble into prayer
as I implore even one of my children
to stand beside me,
give back a bit of the strength
I bequeathed them.

Ashes to Ashes

Ashes tickle my toes and I know
it's a lover wearing a different mask.
We were intended forever
but now his shy kindness follows me
gardenias trailing decadent scent.

Another beloved appears only at night
wringing sweat from my dreams,
assuring me I will wake with first light,
my journey unspooling before me
on belay.

Metaphors nuding avatars, passionate
lure in exuberant verbs
fill my crowded ears.
Each buoyed the other's hesitant step
though hers were few and mine in disarray.

I swallow those soft footsteps through
the depth of this sinuous canyon
and take a chance meeting at my side:
confirming the weight of banishment
so long after what she told me then.

Some whisper, some nudge, some reveal
a map of river stones.
I have no power to quiet them
as they play with eternity
and I still nurture questions here.

These echoes of friends walk with me.
Each brings seductive words,
the message a gift as needed
as when our flesh communed
and living dreams sparked fire.

A Risk Worth Taking

Running away from yourself
you may go too far
and land before you were born.

Think you've been plagued
by confusion
and faced with difficult times?

Imagine searching everywhere
for the moment of your birth
on a landscape scrubbed clean

of the event. Or one that has
never experienced
its definitive statement.

Bereft without yourself, even
a schoolmate's taunt
or the one rejection that mattered

would be welcome now. Loyalty
isn't too much to ask
where you are concerned.

Stay the course, be tolerant
and kind to yourself
and others too. It's a risk worth taking.

Tongue Seeking Solace

for Roberto Tejada, as I ponder his
Still Nowhere in an Empty Vastness

A word is uttered. Its echo dances
through time
and cannot be taken back.
Its silhouette expands
across this map
filling every secret corner.

Breath explodes against rock,
early morning dew
beads upon your lip.
You taste salt
as your tongue seeks solace
between your teeth.

This word was meant to follow
in the wake of that.
Feeling remains
the better part of mind.
We grab as much
as we can hold.

Ancestors drag us back
in *cuenta regresiva*
from that stone notch
where the sun's dagger
meets a future
we do not dare to dream.

Can we inhabit simultaneity
of time and place,
imagine
parting the waters
one more time
to reach where we have been?

What Isn't Possible but Happens

It's morning and the sun came up
again today,
illuminating streets, trees, the roadrunner
who hops onto our front porch
in friendly communion.

I am shuffled into a narrow metal tube
relegated to a seat
for which I have paid extra to bring along my knees
and the whole container rises into the air,
no questions asked.

Food comes scrubbed and packaged without memory
of field or forest,
the kill as distant from this story
as we remain from the hunger of those
who cannot predict their next meal.

These automatic events, these ruptures
between what isn't possible
but happens
mock the meaning of life
in daily doses.

I am fat where I should be muscled and spare,
anxious when wind should be enough,
speak a language
searching for its roots
in every unfamiliar place.

The Rest Was History

for Barbara

Where the trail narrows
overgrown by brush,
where it disappears
into a thicket of juniper and sage,
you are catching up with the others:
those who sang
in your childhood ears,
noticed you in middle school
and knew there was something
terribly wrong when you
went home each night,
but couldn't say the words back then.

It would take decades and
by that time other voices
raised their melodies of safety
or warning rattles.
By then
you knew the difference,
could distinguish
between those who offered
a hand
and those whose hands
went where they had no right
to be.

The rest was history—indelible—
and you made it yours,
made it the canvass

for what your eyes saw
and imagination drew
from a darkness that could easily
have swallowed you whole.
It did not swallow you
and that is your survival,
all yours on a journey
that astonishes now
as it carries your power home.

We Won't Take Yes for an Answer

We tell them no means no
and ask
what part of that word
they don't understand.

Every secret place on the far side
of casual conversation
disappears
after the fire sale.

I would tell you *read my lips*
but fear being taken
for a president
boasting Mission Accomplished.

There is no mission here,
just vulnerability
donning its invisibility cloak
of shame.

We tell them no means no.
They smile disarmingly.
We won't take yes for an answer
and turn them into pillars of salt.

Many Moons

for Mike Moye

It's been fifty years. Do we know
if the flag is still there
or if Armstrong's tread remains
imprinted in the lunar dust?

As with the archaeology at Ephesus
or Machu Picchu,
modern-day looters
vie with the graverobbers of old.

They drill nighttime holes
in mounds of earth
and flood a smuggler's market
with items of metal, gems and clay.

Today the journey itself is for sale,
private enterprise's competitive
race to that sea
euphemistically named Tranquility.

Universal law is never binding
and *one small step for a man,*
one giant leap for mankind
may not get to keep its copyright.

It all depends on where we place
the emphasis: on dubious nouns,
scientific mastery
or today's poor patriotism.

Meanwhile the race is on to Mars
and here on earth
migration isn't measured in vast distances
but human bodies face down in water.

Do we cherish history's artifacts
or pay attention now
to mouths frozen open
hungering for sustenance and truth?

Molecules Sometimes Wonder

"No ideas but in things..."
William Carlos Williams

Beneath the seconds I hear a clock ticking
in a language I once knew.
Beneath the minutes, pathways fade
on frayed maps, their faces turned
to a sputtering midnight sun.
The hours are weighted with surplus food,
the sort that comes in UN packaging,
pale blue with white letters:
desperate invitation to survival.

I carry those days and weeks and months
on a back bent by the poundage of hope
in a world still moving only in one direction:
forward, although its molecules
sometimes wonder whether they are
coming or going.
We press time for new possibilities,
intuit a future long gone
or just around the corner.

I may claim our past
will rise again
or all time is simultaneous
rather than sequential.
I can imagine realities as impossible
as the airplane in 1850
or computers back when I longed
for my first Royal portable.
I can play da Vinci to your doubting Thomas.

But that won't provide the extra year
a woman with cancer hopes she has
or the food needed by a child of war
so she may reach adulthood.
Imagined time still meets
the mundane cousin standing in its way
with broad shoulders,
arms akimbo and all the ballast
of a 390-pound running back.

When it comes to assessing matter,
the movement of atoms, quarks,
string theory, loops, the singularity
at the center of a black hole
or where we are going or have been,
there is only our body's story
etched in a mind that is also flesh,
the perfect location
when approached from all directions.

Divine Love

I was an infant, trusted
life, the people
who cared for me,
food, fresh air, warmth.

Then something happened.
No, didn't happen
but was perpetrated
upon me

by the grandfather
everyone called
a Saint: minister
in one of those cults

organized with men
at the top,
priests and rabbis
doing their dirty work

and women on the
receiving end
even when his church
was founded by a woman.

There is no matter
in Divine Love
her scripture said
and he used and abused

my matter, maybe
telling himself
his love was divine.
It wasn't for me.

Progress

It used to be a blank piece of paper
its edge just visible
above the typewriter's rubber roller
or beckoning on a desk
accompanied only by pencil or pen.

Now the empty rectangle stares
from a backlit screen
we call a monitor
perhaps because it monitors
our efforts to fill it

with ideas never expressed before,
words organized in new ways,
fiction so real it will replace
what you see with your eyes,
hear with your ears.

Along the top of this digital page
infinite choices are offered:
typeface and font size, line spacing,
margin and indentation,
regimented or ragged block of text.

All this may help set the scene
or intimidate as we prepare
to write the narrative
that will allow us
to keep on facing each new page.

We may celebrate the death
of white-out, no more
messy carbon or ugly smudges,
time saved with cut and paste,
spellcheck at our beck and call.

Yet paper or digitally generated,
it's still a blank page.
We still face emptiness
on our way to filling it
and changing history.

Each Toy Argues its Future

Training begins emphatic
and early
with nurseries painted pink or blue.

Each toy argues its
future identity:
fighter planes or dolls

so men will learn to attack
and women
receive their blows.

A proper education continues
as children of all genders
are taught to stay

within the lines. Each number
calls forth a color,
each obedience a round of applause.

And what's this about other genders?
They assure us only two
are sanctioned by God and Flag.

Patriots follow the piper's tune,
gamble on
short-term satisfaction.

Meanwhile, those ready to leap
off that safe and rigid map
discover we are the toymakers.

Mirrors Cut to Size

Norma Jean forever Marilyn:
her crown of spun gold
seductive lips
and innocent eyes
beckoning eternal come-on.

She pouts on the wall of a barber shop
where no natural blonde
has ever gotten a haircut or shave.
We breathe her glamorous allure,
never her fear.

Che's countenance: the single star
on black beret, his wistful eyes
searching a distance
of elusive justice
echoed on a million T-shirts.

We see David facing Goliath,
never asthma in wet grass,
hunger circled by betrayal,
the desperate loneliness
of that fatal ambush.

Perception is everything,
sex impossible
for Jesus of Nazareth,
his mother too depicted
as immaculate.

The blood of his crucified agony
painted by centuries of artists
while Mary Magdalene
remains in a shadow
of sexual shame.

And he is our savior, King
of kings,
Lord of lords,
never the poor carpenter
turned political hopeful.

Mohamed Ali, Tupac Shakur,
Gandhi or Lady Gaga
represent us
in a perfection we cannot embody
on our own.

These are the faces we insist
tell us who we are,
the faces we've erased
to reimagine
in mirrors cut to size.

The Hole October Leaves

I open my eyes and October is gone.
She ducked out while I slept
taking a birthday
and twenty boxes of Girl Scout cookies
a preteen was selling
door to door.

The hole October's left has ragged edges,
a coastline where the struggle for justice
stands on shifting sands
before it succumbs
to fortune tellers
lying through rotten teeth.

There are rules, the big men say,
and they must be followed.
No room for an idea
that sets its own place
at table, does its own dishes,
makes its own bed.

To those who say that's woman's work,
the joke's on you.
Generations fold October's hologram
in sweaty hands,
hold within it the only answer
tough enough to last.

I close my eyes for a second
that feels like centuries:
the loneliness of a hospital ward
where 40 women long to hold
their newborns, Columbus stumbling
upon an inhabited continent,

John Brown's stand at Harper's Ferry,
Trujillo painting the Massacre red,
Ho Chi Minh entering Hanoi,
Che at the Yuro Ravine
and I still trapped
at Tlatelolco.

October is gone. I look to
all the horizons
thinking I catch sight
of a moving shadow
but only the calendar's empty page
stares back.

Above the Bloody Strings

Chile, 1973-2015

The earthquake off Chile's long coastline
measured Richter 8.4 today.
That sinuous shore trembled between desert, surf
and villages of brightly painted houses
facing the silence of numbed memory.

Forty-two years ago, September 16th shuddered
as faceless criminals
broke Víctor Jara's urgent song,
shattered wrists poised above the bloody strings
of his resilient guitar.

One date careens against another
and, if we listen, we can hear
a resonant echo, a hologram
of sound where redemption
hides its face in shame.

Democracy

For Conchita it's a synonym for
this country to the north.
She knows she will risk her life
on the journey, might not
make it across a border
where only myth keeps dreams alive
despite reports of camps
where her baby
may be taken from her arms.

She cannot know that even if she
reaches her destination
she will still be dark-skinned
foreign and female,
that language and custom
will hover beyond her reach.
She does not know that democracy
is reserved for natives
but not the real natives.

What were those Athenians thinking
1,500 years ago?
Aristotle's vision of citizen representation
ringing a bell for equality
but women and slaves
weren't citizens,
justice was limited by class and gender,
a practice we continue to refine
to meet our modern-day goals.

An institution only for those
who speak English
without an accent
even if *alien*, *nigga* and *faggot*
rise like bullies on their tongues,
and especially for those with money
because despite its reputation
democracy is mostly for those
who do not need its promise.

When It Comes to Rights

When the idea of a good war
rises in me
Spain appears waving a flag,
international brigades in broken return,
the last good war
as if there've been none since.

When the word *disappeared* erodes
on my lips and tongue
I am not thinking of a sixth extinction
but of humans, members
of our own species
plucked from streets and homes.

When someone says *commodity*
I see the repeated images
of a Campbell's soup can,
Marilyn Monroe on a grid of squares
chiding a conscience
receptive to suggestion.

And when art claims my emotion
I reach all the way back
to the hidden walls of caves,
forward to cold lofts, 1950s New York,
or murals that still speak
our history and desire.

When it's music, Thelonious nestles
in my inner ear,

strains of Willie Nelson
poke through summer grass,
a future of Ferron and Kate Wolf
wait to caress raw edges.

And when it comes to rights
I believe they are all mine
as surely as I was born a woman
and queer
in an age that still fears
who I am.

Blame it on the Kid

Sure, blame it on the kid:
El Niño, as if
he caused the whole mess
and it's not a matter
of bad rearing.
Spare the rod, spoil the child
doesn't explain
this twenty-first century dilemma
serious enough to do us in.

It's easy to blame homelessness
on sloth, rape on
provocation, war on a fabricated story
of weapons of mass destruction.
El Niño: result not reason
for a sizzling earth, our children
growing up to find they belong
to the first generation that will not
live better than the one before.

In the Gaze of a Clear Eye

for the unidentified young man who stood
in protest in front of a column of tanks
leaving Tiananmen Square on June 5, 1989

Legions marched with blinded eyes
to a worn but patriotic beat
legs goose-stepping in unison
breasts swollen with manufactured pride.

Cotton candy's bright pink
spun out of control,
reduced to a lump
too viscous to swallow.

Among the regiments one hundred
by one hundred on each side,
a single figure turned and moved
in the opposite direction.

We could not tell if man or woman,
androgynous or simply too far
away for us to satisfy
our need to label and define.

Out of step with community and nation
challenging the authoritarian code
all eyes followed
the one who would not follow.

The patriotic music stopped and each of us
could hear her own heartbeat

sounding through our bodies
in empowering harmony.

Sweet mountain air returned
to every lung.
Hands came alive
with making and doing.

One hundred years passed
in one quickened breath.
Everyone followed
the odd one out

and everyone's integrity was safe
for one more eon
passing like an instant
in the gaze of a clear eye.

Love and Let Love

You said I love you in 1952
looking nervously
side to side—
did anyone hear or see?
Blood escaped your lips,
rushed to your cheeks,
flooded a brain alert to danger
and careful to keep the secret
cowering in your veins.

You say I love you in 2020
and the words lift
their eyes, stretch their arms.
Your person smiles
and kisses you
on a busy street
by a park where children
run and play
their own games of desire.

Imagine how much pain
we could avoid
if we fast-forwarded
every consensus
to love and let love
in this slow-motion world
burdened by the fears
of those afraid to open their eyes
and greet tomorrow.

Bed

is where we lay our bodies down,
upscale futon
with solid foam core.
A warm comforter shrouding my feet
in winter, light touch of fresh white cotton
when the season turns.
And you are there beside me
even when I am alone in some hotel room
traveling with poetry, suspending my longing
against a plummeting temperature.

But something happens as sleep descends.
Doesn't matter what I had for dinner
or what position I curl my ageing body in.
Elevators won't stop
on the right floor, taxis race
through tangled streets, the slow motion
of hurrying to make a plane
before they close the gate, get to
a job on time, rescue a loved one
before the paramilitaries come.

Flashes of blood-streaked skin, erratic lights
startle terrified eyes, nameless images
careen through time and space.
Escape is out of breath.
Solutions that aren't solutions
move my body but leave my spirit
behind. Words are not permitted
here. Words are not permitted.

Believe me, I would use them
if they were.

Numbed to the Action on the Ground

My memory was all but
battered into silence,
made thin and sparse
as it crossed the 17th parallel
clinging to my hand.

It didn't make it aboard those helicopters
lifting off the embassy roof
in a city renamed
Ho Chi Minh,
but scarred with pictures

filling our TV screens, trying
to balance their impact
with what it had heard
from mothers and sisters
about why the fighting stopped.

When we abandon them
our memories corrode
in a swamp sewn with guilt
or numbed to the action
on the ground.

Now I retrieve my memory
from where it cowers,
fold it neatly
or place it in my closet
on a hanger of bent wire.

I've never sent it out to be cleaned,
wash it gently by hand,
yet human eyes
catch sight of the stains
bestowed by history books.

They tell the wrong stories
then walk away,
confident no one will notice,
question their credibility
or catch them in their lies.

My memory notices. It speaks
with the sure voice of age,
pronounces each word
like the images it saw
and recorded so long ago.

Memory, Photographic and Otherwise

A few hesitant snapshots
hide their faces guiltily,
others maintain equilibrium
through these 84 years,
revealing a friend
whose face
I no longer remember.

Some scenes embrace me
in steady company,
others leap from the trail
when a torrent of water
roars through a narrow canyon
or shrivel to dust
where rain abandons the *tinajas*.

Some photos are cracked or frayed
but continue to bring
into fragile focus
where I have been and why.
Others document events
that never happened:
holograms of desire.

These clues, mysterious or definitive,
reach out to take me by the hand,
overcome weariness,
impatience and lies.
They know they still have work to do
along pathways that have yet
to reach the cliff's edge.

Pristine in Exotic Memory

Names like *Able* and *Bikini* still ride the crests of waves,
pristine in exotic memory.
For the good of mankind we told the victims
forced to neighboring atolls.

But the explosion pulverized coral, and snowflakes
traveled south on ashy winds,
writing a new narrative of deformed bodies,
cancerous legacy.

I ask who matters? Trayvon, Watchful Bear, María,
their histories scraping the fracked rock
of a nation attacking all
who reach our gap-toothed borders.

The darker the skin or more slanted the eyes,
more precarious the fit—*Your tired,*
your poor, your huddled masses
now a promise abandoned in eroding stone.

Fashioned of Blood and Memory

I already miss books, printed and bound
with an eye to heft, malleability,
design and how they feel in the hand,
texture of paper, scent of ink.

I wander from hand-illumination to Guttenberg,
hot lead and letterpress to digital,
tradeoffs where quality always loses
to cost-effective, gimmick replaces spine.

When they kill hand-crafted books, they will
have taken the silence between our words
imagination's mystery catching that light
that floods beneath a door.

You say not in our lifetime, but I remember
the prop plane, eggbeater, rotary phone,
my own left hand signaling out the rolled down
window of a car in winter.

Each new invention a time- or energy-saver
making life more expedient, perhaps
more fun. But something is lost, something
fashioned of blood and memory.

Imagine This

Imagine a large sieve,
metal mesh wide
as a football field
where memories are spooned
across the top.
The purest, the heaviest
fall through. The chaff
remains.

The most valuable memories
born just before birth
or in those final moments of life
when all external images dim
and what matters most
settles deep and forever
taking pride of place
at a moment that knows no equal.

Imagine a wind, gentle or hearty,
blowing away what didn't
make it through,
and what falls, journeying
to some great communal pot
where history is made.
Imagine this in a dimension
we have yet to dream.

Memories divided into fact
or fantasy,
become our past
or fly headlong toward the sun
until they are consumed
in the heat of illusion.
Then imagine this in a dimension
beyond time.

With Memory Clinging to My Back

My memory taps me
on the shoulder,
boasts it is longer
and sharper than I.

It brings up 1959,
the revolution
in Cuba had just
been victorious

and I'd begun to think about
creating justice
in a world where justice
must fight subterfuge.

That year an editor told me
my novel was no good,
suggested I go home,
marry and have some kids:

advice given to women
back then
whether our dream
was doctor or poet.

My memory reminds me
that was the moment
my life appeared to split.
I saw revolution

and art wandering
separate paths
and struggled to
pull them together:

not wife and mother or
poet and revolutionary
but all of the above
because I never doubted

I would do it all, fail
then do it better,
memory always
clinging to my back.

Those Memories We've Forgotten

for Cedar Sigo

At 10 I was terrified when lies rose
among the blades of grass
waving their treacherous arms
and threatening
to suck the breath
from between my teeth.

At 24 the tiny animals that lived
beneath my breastbone
began to wander in different directions.
Some struggled to gain altitude
while others hoped no one noticed them
sheltering in place.

They took the warnings seriously,
wanted to stay
on the right side of history.
But what is the right side of history?
By the time I was 47
camouflage had lost its appeal.

Sun wasn't slanted right for the shadow
I kept pasted to my foot.
We slip in and out
of the stories they tell
in our name,
fear our deepest intuitions.

At 84 none of this matters.
Earth is on course
to shed us like dry skin,
and you who are 10 or 24 or 47
must take care to preserve
those memories we've forgotten.

Where All that is Forgotten Lives

Island or hideout beneath the stairs,
there is a place
where all that is forgotten lives.
It is learning a second language,
does not communicate
easily.

I knock on its door, sometimes
greeted by silence
or hear murmured conversation
meant for younger ears.
Bomb blasts replaced by the drone
of permanent war.

If you believe you can hunt
elusive thoughts
or words with assault weapons
you do not know your prey.
If you resort to force
the object

of your desire will disappear
in aging eyes.
Only the tenderest hand
can reel it in:
bodies barely touching
in the night.

Memory and Echo Play Together in a Modern-Day Garden of Eden

Memory and Echo play together in
a modern-day Garden of Eden
where only invisible flowers bloom
and someone is designing a fountain
for every season.

Such gardens appear here and there
at the bleakest of times,
ready to welcome those who survive
exploitation, false promises
and patriarchal deception.

Echo brings us the strains of spirituals
sung on ghost ships
crossing the Atlantic
packed with the bodies of slaves
dreaming of their African home.

She carries the cries of natives
forced to leave their lands
and march west, the sighs of women
through centuries of grief,
dependence and subservience.

Memory takes Echo's hand, asks for
this dance and all future dances
along garden paths
that welcome an era in which
every flower grows.

The Big Prize

The invitation comes on embossed paper
costing two trees their lives
although no evidence remains
of how such old growth came to occupy
the matching envelope.

Suggested formal dress precludes
attendance by your children,
next-door neighbor
or the beloved mentor who
first encouraged you to write.

Family would have to travel
halfway around the world,
paying their own way
to hear you proclaimed
what they've always known.

This great honor that might have
boosted your confidence
at forty, changed your life
at fifty or sixty,
at eighty brings dilemma.

Not the first woman or lesbian
or lover of justice,
no longer unique or surprising
but still among the 1%
of those who win today,

you carry in your blood
the memory of all
who have been denied:
told in a way that threatens
who you are.

Will you take the money and run
or use the occasion to deliver
a carefully worded protest
against the politics so perfectly
embodied in this prize?

When is *one against the world*
the way to go?
When is your deviant voice
yours alone
shattering a silence of centuries?

Finite Distance Stumbles

I observe your smallest
muscles, how tight
or relaxed they are,

notice the hummingbird
hovering
outside our window.

Do her wings beat
faster or
slower than before?

Uncertainty in stark relief
when time
is woven of questions:

I write focus in
fading ink,
loneliness in italics.

Finite distance stumbles from
door to table, from
where I stand to a future

gripped by the music
of wings
moving to imagination's beat.

Tango

Thumbs dance a graceful tango
as right moves left
and left returns across keys
in deliberate journey.

I look at the pianist's feet
upon the pedals,
automatic underpinning,
cellular memory.

I observe the energy rising
from his center
through perpendicular torso,
hands exploding unrelenting hope.

I search his eyes oblivious
to mine
because they already inhabit
a destination beyond time.

That destination's sound
is loyal to a composer
dead before his birth.
The thumb tango lifts me

from my front-row seat,
pulls me into a forest
where black and white move faster
than the speed of gasping breaths

exploding from the lungs
of a patient in Kabul
still burning in her hospital bed
after the US strike.

Collateral damage, the spokesperson
explains
on condition
of anonymity.

Lost Hours

It was never meant to be a City on the Hill
but redemption here on earth,
that new world we were fighting for,
bourgeois mansions
converted into centers
where children marvel at undersea life
or the craters of the moon.

We patrolled our neighborhood's
nighttime hours, broken
buildings and rutted streets,
fierce sea roaring
over the Malecon's low wall,
salt eating sidewalks
and twisting the roots of trees.

The promise was enough rice
for everyone, enough
healing and learning, enough
jobs, and when we could no longer work
a chance to see what
the young ones would do
with what we'd leave to them.

But the promise took everything.
Every fissure became a snare,
no way to replace the time
a mother might have spent with her child,
a father's weekends free to bat that ball.

Where are those lost hours now:
their promises ripping our flesh?

When Death Visits

When Death visits a house
she lingers,
hiding in corners and behind doors:
sanctified symbol of loss.

When Death visits a body
away from home,
she may bring a chill in mid-summer
or words stuttering on tired lips.

Death is crafty, chooses
undefended moments
to scratch an itch
you didn't know you had.

She is proud of her work:
She's thorough
and never leaves for tomorrow
what can be accomplished today.

Sometimes she relieves the suffering
of one who has lived too long
or calms the turmoil of another
whose mind can't keep pace with her body.

Sometimes she takes a child: clearly
a mistake. Yes, Death too
makes mistakes, like when she hitches a ride
with a speeding car or in a random bullet.

Sometimes Death wants to dance
a slow waltz or passionate tango.
She may pull you to her
then release you when the music stops.

Uninvited, Death shows up
on her schedule
unmoved by prayer
or the prodigal son who will come tomorrow.

It behooves us to take her calling card,
accept her definitive caress
and balance her confidence
with memory's enduring presence.

Table Talk

Rina Lazo, 1923-2019

Diego and Frida invite a young Rina to dinner
at the Blue House in Coyoacán.
Frida cooks. Diego the master muralist
looks at the young woman, tells her
if she can't eat spicy food
she will never be able
to paint well.

I see them now, seated around that rustic plank,
the two women sizing each other up,
the man's vast belly moving to the rhythm
of his laughter. Rina's tongue, accustomed
to the gentle food of her Guatemala,
vows to meet the challenge,
nurtures a taste for chili, paints well.

Years later Rina says she thinks her mentor
was telling her she must embrace danger
to risk creation. But what if
the Old Frog simply wanted to burn
those lips he expected to savor in time?
What if the proverbs we repeat
are simply idle table talk?

Death Doesn't Close a Door

Janice Gould: 1949–2019

This morning shoots of tender grass
push between your fingers:
signage leaving confusing messages
on tired land
where past tense
has combed its neat farewell.

When you left, you risked
losing your name,
life settled into its final image.
They will whisper *my friend*
who lost her battle with cancer while I
recite your poems and practice breathing.

You matter in the passion of your verb,
the woman you left behind,
your father who became Cynthia then Barbara.
I wonder when they will give prizes
for dignity,
the defiant way you walked.

Death doesn't close a door, your name
remains a fierce marker
pushing your journey before you,
projecting you into forever, holding us
skin to skin, word to word,
one side to the other.

We Move America

for Annette, as she takes flight

In the heat of a mid-summer evening
from the verandah of this old hotel
restored to 1930s glory
before planes silenced these tracks
and rails were the way to travel,
we watch the trains go by.

Duos of orange *engines that could* and can
pull snaking ribbons of freight cars,
one passing every few minutes.
We listen to the clang of coupling
as containers jerk and strain
in silhouette against a monsoon sky.

We Move America proclaim
the TV commercials
as they show us images
—scrubbed and sparkling—
of roaring trains
confident they control our lives

while we catch glimpses of
the automobiles stacked
two tiers high, the tractors,
cement, and surely weaponry:
all our imagination can conjure
as speed blurs or reveals their journey.

Company names are neatly stenciled
on each steel box: *China*, *BNSF*,
Union Pacific, *Ferrocarriles de Mexico*,
Amtrak, *Canadian Pacific*, and *CSX*.
Names that built nations
then faltered as flight replaced the track.

But below those logos of commerce
moving their cargo across our map
each car sports wild graffiti: outsized
lettering, raucous color, a language
daring decipherment,
begging a moment of our time.

Artists who choose the steel siding
as their canvasses,
work quickly, risk arrest,
tag rebellion in vivid color:
courage appearing on the run
challenging our fear.

Through canyons and across plains
a moving gallery of people's art
sends those names of industry
into momentary retreat, moving
America to a place that favors
creativity, denounces greed.

Dead

Dead as in disappeared.
No more,
no less:
absence suffered by those left behind.

For the dead
it is a future
without future,
a place devoid of there.

One parent then another,
a sister and friends:
the fearful staccato
gathering speed as I age.

Questions accompany each departure:
Where is her small square body
hunched over paper
writing "fever tumor" in a poem?

Where has he stashed our drinking water
on the way to Kiet Seel?
Where the unwritten pages of the novel
he left behind?

It doesn't help to understand
that energy
doesn't die
but simply changes form.

Absence: no more,
no less,
such forever absence
of being.

The Phantom Elevator

Although persistent, it isn't even
the worst nightmare.
I'm in an elevator,
sometimes old and rusted,
pieces breaking off and landing
thunderously on distant floors below.
Often the walls
of the cage itself fall away,
disappearing into a bottomless void,
its thunder like bullets in my flesh.

Terror pierces my finger
as it presses each button.
I try to signal a desired floor.
If I've pushed *four*
the machine may creak to a stop
on *nine* or *nineteen*.
My finger tries again, my heart
beats in uneven crescendo,
threatening to stop altogether
as I hurtle past my destination.

Perhaps *nine* isn't so bad
if I'm aiming for *seven*.
I could always descend two floors
on foot, I think, or *nineteen* is fine
if I'm headed to *twenty-two*,
the upward climb would do me good.

But when the elevator stops
and I step out, there are no stairs
or even a landing, only a ferocious wind
threatening to sweep me to oblivion.

Each time I find myself nowhere
my breath turns to ice,
its tiny splinters catch in my throat
and fresh blood
fills my lungs.
I dread this nightmare
more than my own death.
Luckily, I inhabit what is left
of the First World so trust
I will wake from the dream.

My Nightmares

They repeat themselves, these dreams
that rattle and rough me up,
nightmares for which the term
seems pale, inadequate.

I no longer awake from the one in which
a trail bordered by my greatest fear
gets narrower,
suffocating survival

but those where I race to make the flight
to Cuba still charge
through my nights, leaving me
teetering on high wire.

Hunting unsuccessfully for a lost passport
is another frequent nighttime journey.
I am methodical in my search,
slow and diligent even as I know I will fail.

Lately, though, the subject matter
has changed, become
scatological, smelly, every facet
of the dream coated in excrement.

And I mean literal feces, mine,
more desperate and pervasive
than anyone's.
I who take such pride in cleanliness.

As the years pass and life stretches on
there is always another opportunity
for desperation. Even waking
to this new normal promises relief.

The Child Covers Her Eyes

The child covers her eyes
with her small palms,
believes no one
can see her
because she sees no one.

We adults cover our eyes
with ignorance,
a metaphor in these times
when many think
knowledge is sin.

The child is playing
with discovery,
exploring what will
be of use
and what she will discard.

We exercise choice at our peril
or delight. Take a chance:
Know it is possible
to remember the trick
of hands over eyes

even as we fool ourselves
and others,
agree to dance with play
as we struggle
with destruction.

Suspicion and Empty Parables

We are traveling somewhere
but have no map.
The lines on my palm shimmer
as electric current
spiders across pads of flesh
speaking a language no one knows.

There are two of us and then
I am alone, but soon
thousands accompany me
until each disappears
trailing promises made
before they were born.

Carrying the past like that
is a heavy burden,
weighted with suspicion
and empty parables.
Those who can't keep up
burn out like dying stars.

We can still see their light
but know it is a reflection
of something ancient
and cold,
precious in memory
but long gone.

I have always kept a journal,
believed it would serve
those born after I'm gone.
In my dream I see its pages
dissolving in the fire
that's consumed an entire town.

I can no longer crouch
behind the Other.
Famine and fire have swept us
from that mirror
where I once felt
the disingenuous safety of exception.

The Line as Wound

The line as wall, no, the line as wound,
and we wonder if we too are guilty
of escaping into *us* and *them*?
The line itself has its history
of pilfer and disgrace.
We remember 1848:
imperial invasion of another people's land.

The line is wound and also memory:
taking by force, rejecting
by force, condemning
those fleeing misery and brutality
to a new misery and brutality
in the name of false patriotism
until humanity—theirs and ours—

is lost in political babble, children
torn from parents,
desperate men and women
forced into cages
where kindness and compassion
cannot breathe.
We write their history in our shame.

Shy Circles Then Closes In

Shy circles, then closes in
as her years unfold,
creeping up on the woman
whose voice, once righteous and loud,
hit walls and boomeranged,
bouncing back to fill her
with unforeseen dread.

She never expected *Shy*, believed
it to be the burden of others,
that it wouldn't come
to where she stands
firmly defiant and proud
in this world of male privilege,
easy entitlement.

Could it be she mistakes
Thoughtful for *Shy*,
misreads an attribute of choice
for one of shame?
A moment long as life itself
when doubt invades wisdom
and prevails.

Leonardo

"Painting is poetry that is seen rather
than felt, and poetry is painting that
is felt rather than seen."
Leonardo da Vinci

Too big for biographers, we have
only bits and pieces of your life
—the art itself
and your thousands of notes
readable with the aid of a mirror
telling us so much less
than we want to know.

Painter, philosopher, scientist, creator
of lavish events for kings, popes
and other nobility who supported you
despite the sodomy trial
swept under history's rug.
Your search for knowledge, slow work pace
and loneliness all wear us down.

Illegitimate child who never knew
a mother, took solace in nature
and young men,
foretold the bicycle, submarine,
elevator, a flying machine
and locks to raise and lower
the water in Italy's canals.

Court aid proved too sporadic
to ease your days,
commissions too few
to provide a stable income
or the security you needed to create
without concern
for the prejudices of your time.

We invent clues, imbue your works
with meanings they may
or may not have,
imagine stories beneath
those you wrote
with that left hand
some said belonged to the Devil.

Easy for jealousy to speak
of the Devil
when genius moves so far
beyond understanding
and the artist lived and died
five hundred years before
we might have met him eye to eye.

Bringing Takeout to the Curb

written during the
Coronavirus crisis of 2020

Treacherous, determined, invisible, this
new death pushes its way
into churches where congregants
hope to gain God's ear.
It hides on playgrounds, in upscale restaurants,
ravishes hospitals and morgues,
wraps its jaws around those who still believe
it won't touch them or those they love.

Uruguay no longer accepts flights
from the United States,
a country Norway also does not trust.
Cuba takes sick tourists into its hospitals,
caring for them as it does all those in need,
while the madwoman ruling Nicaragua
orders her people to party big
confident God will keep them safe.

Here small cafes and neighborhood shops
bring takeout to the curb,
practice solidarity even as they know
they may not outlive this plague.
Our president saves corporations
too big to fail while telling citizens
to forage for our needs:
capitalist judgement on grotesque display.

I wash my hands a dozen times a day,
cough into my elbow, stay home
but check on vulnerable friends
and imagine a future
where this system of greed and hate
will be cast aside
for one in which we truly care
and act accordingly.

Ignition of Skin on Skin

written during the
Coronavirus crisis of 2020

Virtual touch: the latest oxymoron
in these baffling times.
Locked down in fear vs. locked away
by fascist authority
bears no comparison.
Still, virtual isn't limbic
by any stretch of feeling.

Questions sprout like blades
of spring grass:
In a future of endless quarantine
will mothers and the unborn
enjoy the only bond?
In communities to come
will virtual be the norm?

In a touchless future
will couples
already living together
be the only humans exciting
ignition of skin on skin?
How will pheromones travel
and where will they end up?

What new intimacy can replace
our millennial dance?
How will we find
empathy, compassion, love
without the signposts
hands fashion
on our bodies' map.

We are asked to believe the flight
of a butterfly in Japan
can cause a tornado
in Oklahoma. Will erasure
of so much human touch
bring a new ice age or revive
the balm of tropical rains?

The Trail of Doors

Through the velvet night
I walk a trail of doors:
some majestically ornate
like the lacquered gates
of Peking's Forbidden City
before revolution
rendered them irrelevant,
some small and plain
like the door that led
to a hideout
beneath the stairs
in my childhood home.

Some doors are broad
like those on barns
or old carriage houses,
some ominous such as those
separating witnesses
from the execution chamber.
Some welcome
an anxious traveler,
others seem remote,
not eager to reveal
secrets reserved
for those of a certain age.

But the image of a door closing
enters my fear
like the daily news
or an unidentified twinge of pain
in an aging body,
an unexpected report
—not the kind you want to get—
about a friend you haven't
thought of in years
but still love
or a moment you've always wished
you could take back.

As I walk through one,
then the next,
I understand the message
is that all stand open
and none close behind me
as I cross its threshold.
This tells me
I will be able to return
along the same trail
to the beginning of my dream
and awaken to life again
with all my memories intact.

I Move through His Lies at the Speed of Light

It's been a decade since I ascended
that trail from desert floor
to mountain crest
glowing watermelon red
each breathless
afternoon.

Longer still since I flew
over Bright Angel,
feet barely touching crude steps
of earth descending
to where a river licks the edges
of my canyon.

Today I work so my ups and downs
aren't stuck
between the clenched teeth
of a Bully-in-Chief
who lies to keep us tethered
to his power.

I move through his lies
at the speed of light.
Age has taken my legs
but not my certainty
he is here today,
will be gone tomorrow.

Eight Minutes 46 Seconds

written during the last week of May 2020
when George Floyd, yet another in a long list
of unarmed Black men, was murdered by police.

The time it took for George Floyd to die
beneath the rage of white policemen,
time slowing to silence as his windpipe
collapsed beneath that savage knee.

Emmett lived hours knowing he'd never
see Mama. Time stopped for Trayvon
when he couldn't talk his killer down, and
for Sandra in the cell that became her tomb.

The clock ran out for Eric who knew
his pleadings were useless,
and for the thousands our country lynches
in this take-no-prisoners age.

Together they fall, hands raised before
regulation bullets, law and order
weaponry: bitter fruit swinging
from the branches of shamed trees.

The murderers wear white robes with
pointed hoods or the uniform blues
of our cities' finest. They may be
on or off the job in this "us" and "them"

that turns the racist joke to hate and then
to the war our executioner-in-chief
fuels as he sows and reaps
America's killing fields.

Eight minutes 46 seconds: the time
it takes fear to morph into murder
and democracy to choke on this land
that once pretended equality for all.

I can't breathe...

I forfeited my breath while
he had his way with me,
have spent a lifetime
trying to get it back.

My husband battered me
until I lost five teeth,
lips swollen shut, each breath
a strike of the branding iron.

I live amidst toxic waste.
Every inhalation
takes me closer
to my last.

It's hard to breathe inside
this cardboard shelter,
dreaming about the home
I lost.

When they call me *nigger*,
greaser, *faggot*, *kike* or *slut*,
my breath freezes
into a chokehold of fiery pain.

For the Black men held down
by a white cop's knee
on their neck,
the cry is literal:

I can't breathe... I can't breathe...
until there is no breath left
and they die gasping the song
now a mantra for us all.

Breathe Another Day

for Bill Nevins,
for asking the question.

Poetry, I say, *you let me down,*
remembering
my conviction
she could change the world,
raise consciousness,
right every wrong.

Poetry looks me in the eye
and laughs out loud.
That was asking a lot, she says,
shrugging tired shoulders
and making that little gesture with her lips
that renders my demand absurd.

But you possess a hidden power,
I argue:
recalling Homer, Sappho,
Nezahualcoyotl, Shakespeare,
Sor Juana, Vallejo, Brecht and Whitman:
poets whose words define us,
model the values
by which we hope to live.

And the breakthrough voices:
Langston, Ginsberg, Roque,
Gelman, Rich,
Lorde and Waldman
who shatter established paradigms,
open our eyes to change.

Poetry is less defensive then,
no doubt pleased I've named
her illustrious representatives.
It isn't every day she enjoys
such tribute
in a culture given to hashtags
and emoticons: poor stand-ins
for the richness of language.

Her voice is resonant, neither
battered by age
nor strained by circumstance.
She mentions epics
like Vietnam's "Tale of Kiew"
with its 2,254 verses
and Argentina's "Martín Fierro,"
long poems school kids memorize
one generation to the next

but cautions memorization
can kill memory
—all those times you faltered in class,
had to begin again
with no idea
what the poem was about
or what it had to do with you.

She argues for Surrealism's gaze
born in France and lifting us
into surprise:
Aragón, Artaud, Breton and Eluard,
poets who changed
the way we see. Insists:
Surely they altered our consciousness.

But I tell Poetry I'm talking about
righting the big wrongs:
You know, I say, *systemic change.*
We used to claim poetry—art—
could make a real difference.
What became of that?

That was your claim, not mine,
poetry shrugs.
I never said
I'd change the world,
only that I'm here,
trying my best,
and you might do me the favor
of appreciating me for what I am.

Then I remember Ad Reinhardt's words:
Art is art and everything else
is everything else. It's true,
I asked too much. We need poetry—art—
as balance and counterweight,
a space where hate cannot find its way
or violence bloom in this petri dish
of *us* and *them.*

Poetry interrupts again: *You can't*
expect me to fix the mess
you've made from fear and greed.
That would be placing on my shoulders
a responsibility that's yours
by virtue of your choices and your shame.

Okay, Poetry, I say, *I no longer demand*
the impossible of you.

I'll keep writing and reading you
for what you are:
creativity that lets us breathe
another day.

Postmarked Hanoi

for Roque on the 45th
anniversary of his death.

The letter postmarked Hanoi was written in El Salvador.
The poet told of the people's suffering,
the war in Vietnam wasn't only glory he said,
and I got a whiff of sticky rice wrapped in banana leaves,
faint recall of raisins and cinnamon.

The poet had gone home to fight for his country's liberation
from the monster to the north and its local goons.
He knew *Nicaragua's president was also the president*
of El Salvador and the US president was more the president
of El Salvador than the president of El Salvador.[1]

But he couldn't know his last battle would be with his own
who imprisoned and tortured him, and that he would
lose. Years before, he'd written: *I am acquainted with*
my pain: / I carry it disguised in my blood / and it has cultivated
a special laugh / so no one asks for its shadow.[2]

Someone mailed that letter for him on the other side
of the world to help the poet cover his tracks.
I learned this thirty years later over breakfast
with his son. The father long gone, their country
still small, still sad, still struggling.

---

1 Paraphrase of lines from the poem "O. E. A." from the book *Taberna y otros lugares* (1969).

2 First four lines of the poem "Mi Dolor" from the book *Ventana en el rostro* (1961), translation MR.

My throat constricts as trickster strands of memory
press against it from all sides, promising truth
while they deliver a tale that's outlived its time.
And I wonder about that scent of sticky rice
wrapped in dark leaves, posing as reality.

No words can explain the crime committed
by pseudo revolutionaries unworthy of
the name. Delayed justice cannot erase their villainy
even as we work to bring the assassins to court,
hope to hold them accountable for what they did.

I am asking authentic memory to cut me some slack
and longing for a fresh scent to replace the one
that's lived so long in the folds of a letter whose job
it was to protect a poet inhabiting a place that
would forever be ahead of its time.

My Beginnings and Endings

My beginnings and endings cower within,
hiding in groves of limping muscle,
braving the rapids on rivers of blood
or huddled on islands of fat.

They are fearful they may be seen, taken
at face value or forced to stand guard
as mileposts on backroads
not marked on any map.

But the real problems come when an end
tries to pass itself off as a beginning,
confusing the me who observes
as if from afar

when I am part of the equation, my memory
struggling to reimagine parts
worn through years of indecision:
that moment I should have said no or

cried a full-throated yes as time saw origins
wither, almost die, then rise again,
conclusion too often riding
on their broken wings.

You Know Who You Are. Or Maybe Not

Like memory torn in two by
the weight of ponderance,
that time you turned away
in the middle of my sentence
follows you with its tail
between its legs.

By tail I don't mean what
wags from the back
of dogs and other animals
but the shame
that brings abundance
to a screeching halt.

Faint silhouette or shadow
crying for someone
to fill it with rainbow light,
color outside the lines,
forever missing its sister
in courage.

No going back for that, no
laughter or sigh will
render it whole, no patience
will make it disappear.
You know who you are.
Or maybe not.

In Step with Desire

I always asked questions of the poem,
sometimes even glimpsed an answer
flying off to nurse its broken wing.

Certainty lived between folds of skin:
bright light, or shadow deep
as a black hole in a distant universe.

I measured distance in layers of color
applied with a heavy brush,
held escape in a tight fist.

But in this, my nineth decade, I choke
on those questions: warm milk
promising what it cannot deliver.

Place is change, cold monuments
stand where love once promised
to conquer all.

Entitlement begs to borrow a harness
made of melting ice
tethered to this broken dawn.

My map dissolves beneath storm clouds
as I run between canyon walls
pressing against my wanting.

Each image struggles to find its way
across a quartered landscape
of memory unbound.

Today's questions boomerang,
mock my practiced attempts
to pin them to conviction.

Uncertainty moves through my arteries
calling my name in the minor key
of ancestral catch and release.

But not that uncertainty. Not that one.
Some truths never die:
in step, as they are, with desire.

Delayed Fruit[3]

These succulent Judean dates have history on their side.
From Masada, the desert fortress by the Dead Sea
where Jewish zealots besieged by Romans
chose death over slavery in AD 73.

From seeds dormant for 2,000 years to hands
that nurture cross-border pollination,
from tiny cracks in the soil
to the shy emergence of living shoots.

From memory to dream, stasis to surprise, hands
gather the pollen from a palm named Hannah
and gently deposit it on Methuselah's flowers,
proud male tree also grown from hope.

The new Judean date is born following two millennia
of displacement and war, sorrow and resistance.
Delicious as life itself for those who taste them now
still dreaming of a future peace.

3 Information for this poem comes from "Aided by Modern Ingenuity, a Taste of Ancient Judean Dates" by Isabel Kershner, New York Times, September 7, 2020.

Promising Trouble When I'm Gone

for Kelly Martínez

If I wanted to go, I went. If I wanted
world, I stretched my arms
and waited. I was propelled on
wings of desire the 1950s chokehold
couldn't kill in me.

In my vocabulary yes was always
a better word than no, red
a better color, imagination
the prize. When I met brilliance,
I asked it who to read.

I gave birth for the first time without
fanfare of husband, home or job,
nothing but love and energy
for that child I brought to life,
thunderous and sweet.

Poetry kept me company then, still
moves in my veins, telling me
it will inhabit my mouth
through war and famine:
perfect balm for hungry lips.

Poetry is always here, like my arms
and world and color, helping me
make it through just as those who
came before, standing beside me now,
promising trouble when I'm gone.

Acknowledgments

Some of these poems first appeared—sometimes in earlier versions or in Spanish translation—in *About Place* (Black Earth, Wisconsin), *Bosque Magazine* (Albuquerque, New Mexico), *Chicago Review Online*, *22 Poems and a Prayer for El Paso* (Dos Gatos Press, El Paso, Texas), *Errancia* (National Autonomous University, Mexico City), *Gulf Coast Journal (*Houston), ISTA (Monevideo, Uruguay), *Tricontinental Newsletter*, *The Blue Nib* (Dublin, Ireland), and *The Zingara Poetry Review.* A number of them, translated into Spanish by Katherine M. Hedeen and Víctor Rodríguez Núñez, were included in *El lenguaje del tiempo* (El Angel Editor, Quito, Ecuador, 2019) and *Espejos cortados a la medida* (Caza de Libros, Bogotá, Colombia), both published in 2019.

Once again, I want to express my gratitude to Bryce Milligan who is a brilliant editor and book designer as well as a dear friend. He has curated my poetry for many years, and it is better for that.

About the Author

Margaret Randall is a feminist poet, writer, translator, photographer and social activist. She is the author of over 150 books. She is the recipient of the 2019 Haydée Santamaría Medal from Casa de las Americas in Havana, and the prestigious 2019 Poet of Two Hemispheres Prize, presented by Ecuador's Poesía en Paralelo Cero. In 2017, she was awarded the Medal of Literary Merit by Literatura en el Bravo, Chihuahua, Mexico. The University of New Mexico granted her an honorary doctorate in letters in 2019. In 2020 she was given the George Garrett Award by AWP and the Paulo Freire Prize by Chapman University.

Born in New York City in 1936, she has lived for extended periods in Albuquerque, New York, Seville, Mexico City, Havana, and Managua. Shorter stays in Peru and North Vietnam were also formative. In the 1960s, with Sergio Mondragón she founded and co-edited *El Corno Emplumado / The Plumed Horn,* a bilingual literary journal which for eight years published some of the most dynamic and meaningful writing of an era. Robert Cohen took over when Mondragón left the publication in 1968. From 1984 through 1994 she taught at a number of U.S. universities, most often Trinity College in Hartford, Connecticut.

Randall was privileged to live among New York's abstract expressionists in the 1950s and early '60s, participate in the Mexican student movement of 1968, share important years of the Cuban revolution (1969-1980), the first three years of Nicaragua's Sandinista project (1980-1984), and visit North Vietnam during the heroic last months of the U.S. American war in that country (1974).

Her four children—Gregory, Sarah, Ximena and Ana—have given her ten grandchildren and two great-grandchildren. She has lived with her life companion, the painter and teacher Barbara Byers, for the past 34 years. When marriage equality was legalized in 2013, they were able to wed.

Upon Randall's return to the United States from Nicaragua in 1984, she was ordered to be deported when the government invoked the 1952 McCarran-Walter Immigration and Nationality Act, judging opinions expressed in some of her books to be "against the good order and happiness of the United States." The Center for Constitutional Rights defended Randall, and many writers and others joined in an almost five-year battle for reinstatement of citizenship. She won her case in 1989.

In 1990 Randall was awarded the Lillian Hellman and Dashiell Hammett grant for writers victimized by political repression. In 2004 she was the first recipient of PEN New Mexico's Dorothy Doyle Lifetime Achievement Award for Writing and Human Rights Activism.

Recent non-fiction books by Randall include *To Change the World: My Life in Cuba* (Rutgers University Press), *More Than Things* (University of Nebraska Press), *Che On My Mind,* and *Haydée Santamaría, Cuban Revolutionary: She Led by Transgression* (both from Duke University Press). Her most recent nonfiction works are *Only the Road / Solo el Camino: Eight Decades of Cuban Poetry* (Duke University Press, 2016) and *Exporting Revolution: Cuba's Global Solidarity* (Duke University Press, 2017).

"The Unapologetic Life of Margaret Randall" is an hour-long documentary by Minneapolis filmmakers Lu Lippold and Pam Colby. It is distributed by Cinema Guild in New York City.

Randall's most recent collections of poetry and photographs are *Their Backs to the Sea* (2009), *My Town: A Memoir of Albuquerque, New Mexico* (2010), *As If the Empty Chair:*

Poems for the Disappeared / Como si la silla vacía: poemas para los desaparecidos (2011), *Where Do We Go from Here?* (2012), *Daughter of Lady Jaguar Shark* (2013), *The Rhizome as a Field of Broken Bones* (2013), *About Little Charlie Lindbergh and other Poems* (2014), *Beneath a Trespass of Sorrow* (2014), *Bodies / Shields* (2015), *She Becomes Time* (2016), *The Morning After: Poetry and Prose in a Post-Truth World* (2017), *Against Atrocity* (2019), and *Starfish on a Beach: The Pandemic Poems* (2020) all published by Wings Press. *Time's Language: Selected Poems (1959-2018)* was published by Wings Press in 2018. Many of Randall's collections of poetry have been published in Spanish translations throughout the hemisphere.

Among Randall's most recent books, her memoir *I Never Left Home: Poet, Feminist, Revolutionary* was published by Duke University Press, and a companion volume, *My Life in 100 Objects* came out from New Village Press, both in 2020.

Wings Press was founded in 1975 by Joanie Whitebird and Joseph F. Lomax, both deceased, as "an informal association of artists and cultural mythologists dedicated to the preservation of the literature of the nation of Texas." Publisher, editor and designer since 1995, Bryce Milligan is honored to carry on and expand that mission to include the finest in American writing—meaning all of the Americas, without commercial considerations clouding the decision to publish or not to publish.

Wings Press intends to produce multi-cultural books, chapbooks, ebooks, recordings and broadsides that enlighten the human spirit and enliven the mind. Everyone ever associated with Wings has been or is a writer, and we know well that writing is a transformational art form capable of changing the world, primarily by allowing us to glimpse something of each other's souls. We believe that good writing is innovative, insightful, and interesting. But most of all it is honest. As Bob Dylan put it, "To live outside the law, you must be honest."

Likewise, Wings Press is committed to treating the planet itself as a partner. Thus the press uses as much recycled material as possible, from the paper on which the books are printed to the boxes in which they are shipped.

As Robert Dana wrote in *Against the Grain,* "Small press publishing is personal publishing. In essence, it's a matter of personal vision, personal taste and courage, and personal friendships." Welcome to our world.

WINGS PRESS

COLOPHON

This first edition of *Out of Violence into Poetry*, by Margaret Randall, has been printed on 60 pound "natural" paper containing a percentage of recycled fiber. Titles have been set in Charlemagne and Caslon Semibold type, the text in Adobe Caslon type. This book was designed by Bryce Milligan.

On-line catalogue and ordering:
www.wingspress.com
Wings Press titles are distributed to the trade by the
Independent Publishers Group
www.ipgbook.com
and in Europe by Gazelle
www.gazellebookservices.co.uk

Also available as an ebook.

For more information about Margaret Randall,
visit her website at www.margaretrandall.org.